General Knowledge – page 2
Transfers Part One – page 6
Cup Games – page 9
Memorable Games – page 11
Red Cards – page 13
Managers – page 15
First Goals – page 17
Transfers Part Two - page 20

General Knowledge Answers – page 24
Transfers Part One Answers – page 29
Cup Games Answers – page 33
Memorable Games Answers – page 36
Red Cards Answers – page 39
Managers Answers – page 42
First Goals Answers – page 44
Transfers Part Two Answers – page 46

General Knowledge

1) Charlie Daniels scored the Match of the Day Goal of the Month for August 2017 against which team?

2) In the 2008/09 season Bournemouth avoided relegation out of the Football League despite starting the season with how many points deducted?

3) Darren Anderton scored a spectacular late winner in his final game as a professional footballer in a match versus which team in December 2008?

4) Artur Boruc saved a penalty from which Manchester United player in the 1-1 draw at Old Trafford in May 2017?

5) Bournemouth started the 21st century by losing away to which team on the 3rd of January 2000?

6) Which company was the club's main shirt sponsor during their first season in the Premier League in 2015/16?

7) Who was the club's top scorer in the 2013/14 Championship season, scoring 22 goals?

8) Who scored for the club aged just 17 years and 1 month in a League One fixture against Gillingham in December 2006?

9) Who became the first Turkish player to represent the club after signing in 2007?

10) Bournemouth won the Championship in the 2014/15 season with what final points tally?

11) Who made their debut aged just 16 years and 21 days old in an EFL Trophy match in 2009?

12) What shirt number did Steve Cook wear during his time at the club?

13) Simon Francis took over as captain from which player ahead of the 2016/17 season?

14) Which Cherries player volleyed in an own goal during the 2-1 home defeat to Arsenal in November 2018?

15) Who scored a hat-trick within the space of 2 minutes and 20 seconds in the 6-0 win over Wrexham in February 2004?

16) The club were relegated from the Premier League in 2020 despite winning their final league game away at Everton by what score-line?

17) Which young striker scored in ten consecutive games while on loan at Bournemouth during the 2000/01 season?

18) Neil Young played the final game of his long Bournemouth career by coming on as a sub against which side in April 2008?

19) Which team did Bournemouth overcome in the Third Division Play-Off Semi-Final of 2003?

20) After their remarkable escape the previous season, the Cherries were promoted from League Two in 2010, securing their automatic place by winning 2-0 away at which club?

Transfers Part One

1) From which club did Bournemouth sign Stephen Purches in June 2000?

2) Which midfielder arrived from non-league side Bashley in February 2000?

3) Luton Town signed which two players from Bournemouth in the summer of 2000?

4) Bournemouth brought in which player from Bordeaux in August 2001?

5) Which player was sold to Portsmouth in March 2002?

6) Warren Cummings joined on a free transfer from which Premier League side in 2003?

7) Bournemouth sold which player to West Ham in the summer of 2004?

8) Which two players moved to Burnley in May 2005?

9) From which team was Conal Platt signed in May 2006?

10) Who was sold to Doncaster Rovers in May 2006?

11) Darren Anderton joined in September 2006 from which side?

12) Steve Fletcher left the club in June 2007 to sign for which club?

13) Which player joined from Celtic in the summer of 2007?

14) Which forwarded was sold to Wolves in May 2008?

15) Bournemouth signed which goalkeeper from Peterborough in 2008?

16) From which non-league club was Anton Robinson signed in 2009?

17) Jo Kuffour moved to which team after leaving in 2008?

18) Marc Pugh was purchased from which club in June 2010?

19) Who joined from Woking in the summer of 2010?

20) Which striker was sold to Bristol City in August 2010?

Cup Games

1) Which team knocked Bournemouth out of the League Cup at the Quarter Final stage in both 2017 and 2018?

2) Bournemouth knocked Premier League Blackburn out of the League Cup in the Second Round in 2004 by winning the penalty shoot-out by what score?

3) Who converted the winning penalty for the Cherries in that match?

4) Which non-league club beat Bournemouth in FA Cup First Round in 2005?

5) Who scored the winner in extra time as Brighton were beaten 1-0 in the League Cup Third Round in 2017?

6) Norwich hammered Bournemouth by what score in the League Cup Second Round of 2021?

7) Who scored a hat-trick in the 3-1 victory over Yeovil in the FA Cup Third Round in January 2022?

8) Bournemouth were knocked out of the EFL Trophy at the Round of 16 stage after losing 6-0 to which side in 2011?

9) Bournemouth were knocked out of the EFL Trophy on penalties by which team in the First Round in 2012?

10) Which four teams did the Cherries beat to reach the League Cup Quarter Final in 2014?

Memorable Games

1) Who scored the stoppage time winner in the dramatic 4-3 victory over Liverpool in December 2016?

2) Bournemouth secured their survival and avoided relegation out of the Football League by beating which team 2-1 at home in April 2009?

3) Junior Stanislas scored in the 98th minute to claim a 3-3 draw with which team in the Premier League in November 2015?

4) Bournemouth beat Lincoln City by what score in the 2003 Third Division Play-Off Final?

5) Who scored a hat-trick in the 8-0 demolition of Birmingham at St Andrews in October 2014?

6) Darren Anderton scored a hat-trick in a 5-0 win over which side in League One in February 2007?

7) Which team did Bournemouth beat 6-1 at home in the Premier League in October 2016?

8) The Cherries won the Championship title on the final day of the 2014/15 season by winning 3-0 away against which team?

9) Bournemouth missed out of a Play-Off place in the 2000/01 Second Division after drawing 3-3 with which club?

10) By what score did Bournemouth beat Brighton away from home in April 2019?

Red Cards

1) Who was sent off for Bournemouth as they threw away a two goal lead to draw 2-2 with Coventry in November 2021?

2) Which two players saw red during the 3-1 away loss to Colchester in September 2000?

3) Which player was dismissed during the second leg of the Championship Semi-Final Play-Off loss to Brentford in 2021?

4) Shaun Maher was given his marching orders during a 4-0 home defeat to which club in March 2005?

5) Simon Francis was sent off late on during a dramatic 3-3 draw with which team in the Premier League in January 2017?

6) Which Cherries player was dismissed in the 2-1 away loss to Brentford in September 2004?

7) Adam Barrett was sent off for handball in a League One clash with which club in August 2011?

8) Against which team did Steve Cook receive a straight red for deliberate handball in January 2020?

9) Who was sent off during the FA Cup loss to Blyth in December 2008?

10) Despite seeing Harry Arter sent off, Bournemouth claimed three points in the Championship with a 2-1 home win over which side in April 2014?

Managers

1) Who was the manager of Bournemouth at the beginning of the 21st century?

2) Sean O'Driscoll left in September 2006 to become manager of which club?

3) Who replaced O'Driscoll as the permanent manager of the club?

4) Bournemouth lost 2-0 at home to which team in the final game of Jimmy Quinn's spell as gaffer?

5) Eddie Howe secured his first win as manager with a 3-1 win over which side in January 2009?

6) Who replaced Howe as gaffer when he left to join Burnley in 2011?

7) Dennis Rofe won his only game in caretaker charge by beating which team 2-0 in October 2012?

8) When Howe returned in October 2012, which team did they beat 3-1 in his first home game back in charge?

9) Who became manager after Eddie Howe left again in 2020?

10) Scott Parker oversaw a League Cup victory by what score-line against MK Dons in his first game as manager in July 2021?

First Goals

Can you name the club that these players scored their first goal for the club against?

1) Jermain Defoe
a) **Swindon Town**
b) **Stoke City**
c) **Southend**

2) Wade Elliott
a) **Wycombe Wanderers**
b) **Barnsley**
c) **Tranmere Rovers**

3) Darren Anderton
a) **Scunthorpe**
b) **Chester City**
c) **Wrexham**

4) Danny Hollands
a) **Cardiff City**
b) **Swansea City**
c) **Wrexham**

5) Brett Pitman
a) Aldershot
b) Luton Town
c) Grimsby Town

6) Danny Ings
a) Burnley
b) Fulham
c) Swindon Town

7) Steve Cook
a) Darlington
b) Huddersfield Town
c) Carlisle United

8) Callum Wilson
a) Coventry City
b) Huddersfield Town
c) Birmingham City

9) Dominic Solanke
a) Luton Town
b) Lincoln City
c) Huddersfield Town

10) Jordan Zemura
a) Barnsley
b) Derby County
c) Middlesbrough

Transfers Part Two

1) Which striker was sold to Burnley in August 2011?

2) From which club did Bournemouth buy Steve Cook in the 2012 January transfer window?

3) Simon Francis arrived from which team on a free in July 2012?

4) Ryan Fraser arrived from which Scottish club in January 2013?

5) Who was bought from Charlton in the 2014 January transfer window?

6) Callum Wilson was bought from which team in 2014?

7) Matt Tubbs made the move to which club in January 2015?

8) Which defender arrived from Ipswich Town in the summer of 2015?

9) Who was sold to Newcastle in July 2016?

10) Which two players did Bournemouth sign from Liverpool in the summer of 2016?

11) Eunan O'Kane moved to which club in August 2016?

12) Which striker was sold to Wolves in June 2018?

13) From which Spanish side was Jefferson Lerma bought in 2018?

14) Bournemouth sold which player to Nottingham Forest in July 2018?

15) Which player arrived from Club Brugge in August 2019?

16) Which club did Jermain Defoe sign for after leaving Bournemouth in July 2020?

17) Andrew Surman left to join which team on a free in 2020?

18) Sam Surridge moved to which Championship club in August 2021?

19) Who arrived from Celtic in the summer of 2021?

20) From which club did Bournemouth buy James Hill in the 2022 January transfer window?

Answers

General Knowledge Answers

1) Charlie Daniels scored the Match of the Day Goal of the Month for August 2017 against which team?
Manchester City

2) In the 2008/09 season Bournemouth avoided relegation out of the Football League despite starting the season with how many points deducted?
17

3) Darren Anderton scored a spectacular late winner in his final game as a professional footballer in a match versus which team in December 2008?
Chester City

4) Artur Boruc saved a penalty from which Manchester United player in the 1-1 draw at Old Trafford in May 2017?
Zlatan Ibrahimovic

5) Bournemouth started the 21st century by losing away to which team on the 3rd of January 2000?
Oldham Athletic

6) Which company was the club's main shirt sponsor during their first season in the Premier League in 2015/16?
Mansion

7) Who was the club's top scorer in the 2013/14 Championship season, scoring 22 goals?
Lewis Grabban

8) Who scored for the club aged just 17 years and 1 month in a League One fixture against Gillingham in December 2006?
Sam Vokes

9) Who became the first Turkish player to represent the club after signing in 2007?
Jem Karacan

10) Bournemouth won the Championship in the 2014/15 season with what final points tally?
90

11) Who made their debut aged just 16 years and 21 days old in an EFL Trophy match in 2009?
Jayden Stockley

12) What shirt number did Steve Cook wear during his time at the club?
Three

13) Simon Francis took over as captain from which player ahead of the 2016/17 season?
Tommy Elphick

14) Which Cherries player volleyed in an own goal during the 2-1 home defeat to Arsenal in November 2018?
Jefferson Lerma

15) Who scored a hat-trick within the space of 2 minutes and 20 seconds in the 6-0 win over Wrexham in February 2004?
James Hayter

16) The club were relegated from the Premier League in 2020 despite winning their final league game away at Everton by what score-line?
Everton 1-3 Bournemouth

17) Which young striker scored in ten consecutive games while on loan at Bournemouth during the 2000/01 season?
Jermain Defoe

18) Neil Young played the final game of his long Bournemouth career by coming on as a sub against which side in April 2008?
Walsall

19) Which team did Bournemouth overcome in the Third Division Play-Off Semi-Final of 2003?
Bury

20) After their remarkable escape the previous season, the Cherries were promoted from League Two in 2010, securing their automatic place by winning 2-0 away at which club?
Burton Albion

Transfers Part One Answers

1) From which club did Bournemouth sign Stephen Purches in June 2000?
West Ham

2) Which midfielder arrived from non-league side Bashley in February 2000?
Wade Elliott

3) Luton Town signed which two players from Bournemouth in the summer of 2000?
Mark Stein and Mark Ovendale

4) Bournemouth brought in which player from Bordeaux in August 2001?
Pascal Tetu

5) Which player was sold to Portsmouth in March 2002?
Eddie Howe

6) Warren Cummings joined on a free transfer from which Premier League side in 2003?
Chelsea

7) Bournemouth sold which player to West Ham in the summer of 2004?
Carl Fletcher

8) Which two players moved to Burnley in May 2005?
Wade Elliott and Garreth O'Connor

9) From which team was Conal Platt signed in May 2006?
Liverpool

10) Who was sold to Doncaster Rovers in May 2006?
James O'Connor

11) Darren Anderton joined in September 2006 from which side?
Wolves

12) Steve Fletcher left the club in June 2007 to sign for which club?
Chesterfield

13) Which player joined from Celtic in the summer of 2007?
Paul Telfer

14) Which forwarded was sold to Wolves in May 2008?
Sam Vokes

15) Bournemouth signed which goalkeeper from Peterborough in 2008?
Shwan Jalal

16) From which non-league club was Anton Robinson signed in 2009?
Weymouth

17) Jo Kuffour moved to which team after leaving in 2008?
Bristol Rovers

18) Marc Pugh was purchased from which club in June 2010?
Hereford

19) Who joined from Woking in the summer of 2010?
Harry Arter

20) Which striker was sold to Bristol City in August 2010?
Brett Pitman

Cup Games Answers

1) Which team knocked Bournemouth out of the League Cup at the Quarter Final stage in both 2017 and 2018?
Chelsea

2) Bournemouth knocked Premier League Blackburn out of the League Cup in the Second Round in 2004 by winning the penalty shoot-out by what score?
Blackburn 6-7 Bournemouth

3) Who converted the winning penalty for the Cherries in that match?
Eddie Howe

4) Which non-league club beat Bournemouth in FA Cup First Round in 2005?
Tamworth

5) Who scored the winner in extra time as Brighton were beaten 1-0 in the League Cup Third Round in 2017?
Joshua King

6) Norwich hammered Bournemouth by what score in the League Cup Second Round of 2021?
Norwich 6-0 Bournemouth

7) Who scored a hat-trick in the 3-1 victory over Yeovil in the FA Cup Third Round in January 2022?
Emiliano Marcondes

8) Bournemouth were knocked out of the EFL Trophy at the Round of 16 stage after losing 6-0 to which side in 2011?
Brentford

9) Bournemouth were knocked out of the EFL Trophy on penalties by which team in the First Round in 2012?
Portsmouth

10) Which four teams did the Cherries beat to reach the League Cup Quarter Final in 2014?
Exeter City, Northampton Town, Cardiff City and West Brom

Memorable Games Answers

1) Who scored the stoppage time winner in the dramatic 4-3 victory over Liverpool in December 2016?
Nathan Ake

2) Bournemouth secured their survival and avoided relegation out of the Football League by beating which team 2-1 at home in April 2009?
Grimsby

3) Junior Stanislas scored in the 98th minute to claim a 3-3 draw with which team in the Premier League in November 2015?
Everton

4) Bournemouth beat Lincoln City by what score in the 2003 Third Division Play-Off Final?
Bournemouth 5-2 Lincoln City

5) Who scored a hat-trick in the 8-0 demolition of Birmingham at St Andrews in October 2014?
Marc Pugh

6) Darren Anderton scored a hat-trick in a 5-0 win over which side in League One in February 2007?
Leyton Orient

7) Which team did Bournemouth beat 6-1 at home in the Premier League in October 2016?
Hull City

8) The Cherries won the Championship title on the final day of the 2014/15 season by winning 3-0 away against which team?
Charlton Athletic

9) Bournemouth missed out of a Play-Off place in the 2000/01 Second Division after drawing 3-3 with which club?
Reading

10) By what score did Bournemouth beat Brighton away from home in April 2019?
Brighton 0-5 Bournemouth

Red Cards Answers

1) Who was sent off for Bournemouth as they threw away a two goal lead to draw 2-2 with Coventry in November 2021?
Jefferson Lerma

2) Which two players saw red during the 3-1 away loss to Colchester in September 2000?
Danny Smith and Claus Jorgensen

3) Which player was dismissed during the second leg of the Championship Semi-Final Play-Off loss to Brentford in 2021?
Chris Mepham

4) Shaun Maher was given his marching orders during a 4-0 home defeat to which club in March 2005?
Hull City

5) Simon Francis was sent off late on during a dramatic 3-3 draw with which team in the Premier League in January 2017?
Arsenal

6) Which Cherries player was dismissed in the 2-1 away loss to Brentford in September 2004?
Neil Young

7) Adam Barrett was sent off for handball in a League One clash with which club in August 2011?
Stevenage

8) Against which team did Steve Cook receive a straight red for deliberate handball in January 2020?
Norwich City

9) Who was sent off during the FA Cup loss to Blyth in December 2008?
Brett Pitman

10) Despite seeing Harry Arter sent off, Bournemouth claimed three points in the Championship with a 2-1 home win over which side in April 2014?
QPR

Managers Answers

1) Who was the manager of Bournemouth at the beginning of the 21st century?
Mel Machin

2) Sean O'Driscoll left in September 2006 to become manager of which club?
Doncaster Rovers

3) Who replaced O'Driscoll as the permanent manager of the club?
Kevin Bond

4) Bournemouth lost 2-0 at home to which team in the final game of Jimmy Quinn's spell as gaffer?
Barnet

5) Eddie Howe secured his first win as manager with a 3-1 win over which side in January 2009?
Wycombe

6) Who replaced Howe as gaffer when he left to join Burnley in 2011?
Lee Bradbury

7) Dennis Rofe won his only game in caretaker charge by beating which team 2-0 in October 2012?
Leyton Orient

8) When Howe returned in October 2012, which team did they beat 3-1 in his first home game back in charge?
Tranmere Rovers

9) Who became manager after Eddie Howe left again in 2020?
Jason Tindall

10) Scott Parker oversaw a League Cup victory by what score-line against MK Dons in his first game as manager in July 2021?
Bournemouth 5-0 MK Dons

First Goals Answers

1) Jermain Defoe
   Stoke City

2) Wade Elliott
   Wycombe Wanderers

3) Darren Anderton
   Scunthorpe

4) Danny Hollands
   Swansea City

5) Brett Pitman
   Aldershot

6) Danny Ings
   Swindon Town

7) Steve Cook
   Carlisle United

8) Callum Wilson
   Huddersfield Town

9) Dominic Solanke
Luton Town

10) Jordan Zemura
Barnsley

Transfers Part Two Answers

1) Which striker was sold to Burnley in August 2011?
Danny Ings

2) From which club did Bournemouth buy Steve Cook in the 2012 January transfer window?
Brighton

3) Simon Francis arrived from which team on a free in July 2012?
Charlton Athletic

4) Ryan Fraser arrived from which Scottish club in January 2013?
Aberdeen

5) Who was bought from Charlton in the 2014 January transfer window?
Yann Kermorgant

6) Callum Wilson was bought from which team in 2014?
Coventry City

7) Matt Tubbs made the move to which club in January 2015?
Portsmouth

8) Which defender arrived from Ipswich Town in the summer of 2015?
Tyrone Mings

9) Who was sold to Newcastle in July 2016?
Matt Ritchie

10) Which two players did Bournemouth sign from Liverpool in the summer of 2016?
Jordon Ibe and Brad Smith

11) Eunan O'Kane moved to which club in August 2016?
Leeds United

12) Which striker was sold to Wolves in June 2018?
Benik Afobe

13) From which Spanish side was Jefferson Lerma bought in 2018?
Levante

14) Bournemouth sold which player to Nottingham Forest in July 2018?
Lewis Grabban

15) Which player arrived from Club Brugge in August 2019?
Arnaut Danjuma

16) Which club did Jermain Defoe sign for after leaving Bournemouth in July 2020?
Rangers

17) Andrew Surman left to join which team on a free in 2020?
MK Dons

18) Sam Surridge moved to which Championship club in August 2021?
Stoke City

19) Who arrived from Celtic in the summer of 2021?
Ryan Christie

20) From which club did Bournemouth buy James Hill in the 2022 January transfer window?
Fleetwood Town

If you enjoyed this book please consider leaving a five star review on Amazon

Books by Jack Pearson available on Amazon:

Cricket:

Cricket World Cup 2019 Quiz Book
The Ashes 2019 Cricket Quiz Book
The Ashes 2010-2019 Quiz Book
The Ashes 2005 Quiz Book
The Indian Premier League Quiz Book

Football:

The Quiz Book of Premier League Football Transfers
The Quiz Book of the England Football Team in the 21st Century
The Quiz Book of Arsenal Football Club in the 21st Century
The Quiz Book of Aston Villa Football Club in the 21st Century
The Quiz Book of Chelsea Football Club in the 21st Century
The Quiz Book of Everton Football Club in the 21st Century

The Quiz Book of Leeds United Football Club in the 21st Century

The Quiz Book of Leicester City Football Club in the 21st Century

The Quiz Book of Liverpool Football Club in the 21st Century

The Quiz Book of Manchester City Football Club in the 21st Century

The Quiz Book of Manchester United Football Club in the 21st Century

The Quiz Book of Newcastle United Football Club in the 21st Century

The Quiz Book of Southampton Football Club in the 21st Century

The Quiz Book of Sunderland Association Football Club in the 21st Century

The Quiz Book of Tottenham Hotspur Football Club in the 21st Century

The Quiz Book of West Ham United Football Club in the 21st Century

The Quiz Book of Wrexham Association Football Club in the 21st Century

Printed in Great Britain
by Amazon